How Do T̶h̶e̶y̶ Grow?

From Puppy to Dog

by Jillian Powell

© 2001 White-Thomson Publishing Ltd

Produced for Hodder Wayland by
White-Thomson Publishing Ltd
2/3 St. Andrew's Place
Lewes, East Sussex
BN7 1UP

Editor: Sarah Doughty
Designer: Tessa Barwick
Text consultant: Jessica Buss
Language consultant: Norah Granger

Published in Great Britain in 2001 by Hodder Wayland,
an imprint of Hodder Children's Books.

British Cataloguing in Publication Data
    Powell, Jillian
        From Puppy to Dog. – (How do they Grow?)
        1. Puppies – Development – Juvenile literature. 2. Dogs –
        Physiology – Juvenile literature
        I. Title
        636.7

ISBN 0 7502 3863 1

Printed and bound in Italy by G. Canale & C.S.p.A.

Hodder Children's Books
A division of Hodder Headline Ltd
338 Euston Road, London NW1 3BH

Contents

Words in **bold** in the text can be found in the glossary on page 30.

Puppies are born

A puppy is born. It is the first in a **litter** of puppies. The mother licks her puppy. This helps it to start breathing.

The puppy is tiny and wet. It cannot hear or open its eyes yet. But it can smell and feel its mother.

The puppies start to grow

These puppies are drinking their mother's milk. This helps them grow strong and fight off **germs**.

These puppies have grown bigger. As they grow, their legs become stronger and they can walk.

Becoming active

This puppy is four weeks old. The puppy
learns by using its eyes and ears.
It also has a very good sense of smell.

Puppies love playing together.

They soon get tired and need to sleep.

Growing first teeth

This puppy is six weeks old. It has its **milk teeth** and can start to eat puppy food. It has four small meals a day.

A puppy loves to bite and chew.
This helps to keep its teeth clean and strong.

Ready for a new home

This puppy is eight weeks old and ready to leave its mother. The puppy will need lots of love and care from its new owner.

A new owner must care for a puppy like a new mother. The puppy needs clean bowls of food and water every day.

A visit to the vet

Puppies must visit the vet before they can meet other dogs. The vet checks that the puppy is healthy.

He is giving this puppy a **vaccination**. This will keep it safe from catching diseases when it goes outdoors.

Being outdoors

The puppy can start to explore its new home and go outdoors. The puppy soon knows the smell of its home and its owner.

The puppy loves running and playing.

It needs to have exercise every day.

This helps it to grow strong and healthy.

Playing with toys

Playing with toys helps the puppy to learn.
It likes to show how strong it is by playing
tug of war with its owner.

The puppy loves to chase and catch toys. Its owner throws it a ball to fetch but never sticks or stones. These may hurt the puppy.

Puppy training

The puppy's owner takes it to puppy school.
It meets other puppies here and learns to get
along with them.

A puppy is taught to sit and stay. The puppy understands when its owner is pleased. It also learns to walk on a lead.

Grooming and bathing

A puppy needs to be **groomed** to keep its coat clean and healthy. Its owner brushes out old fur every week.

The puppy licks its fur to keep it clean.
Sometimes it gets its fur very dirty and
needs a bath.

Food and drink

The growing puppy now eats bigger meals twice a day. A puppy needs plenty of clean water, too.

Sometimes, its owner gives a puppy a special treat such as a dog biscuit. A treat can be a **reward** when it is learning.

A puppy becomes a dog

These puppies have grown into young dogs.

Their bodies have grown longer and firmer.

Their legs are longer and stronger too.

A young dog can hear the tiniest sounds.
It sniffs the air where it can pick up
different smells.

Having puppies

This **bitch** is going to have puppies.
She **mated** with a male dog and the puppies
began growing inside her.

After nine weeks the puppies are born. The mother will feed, wash and look after them. Each puppy will grow up to be a strong, healthy dog.

Glossary

Bitch A female dog.

Germs Tiny particles around us that can carry diseases.

Groomed When an animal's fur has been brushed and combed.

Litter All the young animals born to the same mother at the same time.

Mated When a male and female have come together to have babies. A male gives a female a seed which makes a female egg grow into a baby animal.

Milk teeth The first teeth that a baby animal or person grows.

Reward Something that is given when a person or an animal has done well.

Tug of war A game where two sides pull a rope away from each other as hard as they can.

Vaccination An injection given with a needle into the skin. A vaccination protects animals and people from diseases.

Further information

Books

Animal Hospital Little Book of Puppies (BBC Books, 1999)

Caring For Your Puppy: 101 Essential Tips by Bruce Fogle (Dorling Kindersley, 1997)

Dogs (Oxford Firsts series) by Marjorie Newman (OUP, 2000)

Dogs (Pets series) by Michaela Miller (Heinemann Educational, 1997)

Dogs and Puppies (Stick and Stamp series) by Jason Hook (Quarto Children's Books, 2000)

Dogs and Puppies (Usborne First Pets series) by Katherine Starke (Usborne, 1998)

Puppy (See How They Grow series, Dorling Kindersley, 1991)

Video

You and Your Dog Video (Dorling Kindersley) David Taylor

Pets Video (Dorling Kindersley)

The Wonderful World of Puppies Video

Training Puppies Video John Fisher

CD-ROMs

Multimedia Guide to Dogs (Focus)

Websites

www.bbc.co.uk/education/schools
BBC education online provides lots of information on animals and pets including pet fact files.

www.rspca.org.uk
The official site of the Royal Society for the Prevention of Cruelty to Animals (RSPCA), with lots of useful information on pet care.

www.lurch.net/pets.htm
A site which gives you advice about how to care for your pet. It also includes pages on the care of your dog plus games, stories and crafts.

Useful addresses

You can write to the RSPCA for advice on pet care. Remember to enclose an A4 stamped and self-addressed envelope for a reply.

Enquiries service, RSPCA, Causeway, Horsham, West Sussex, RH12 1HG.
Tel: 01403 264181

Index

Picture acknowledgements

Angela Hampton Family Life Picture Library 10, 11, 12, 16, 17, 19, 21, 24, 25, 28; NHPA 7 (E. A Janes), 26 (Yves Lanceau); HWPL title page; Oxford Scientific Films 4 (Liz Bomford), 5 (Clive Bromhall), 6 (Michael Leach), 14 (Daniel J. Cox), 23 (Renee Stockdale/Animals Animals), 27 (Zig Leszczynski/ Animals Animals), 29 (J. L Klein & M. L Hubert/Okapia); RSPCA Photolibrary 8 (Cheryl A. Ertelt), 9 (Cheryl A. Ertelt), 13 (Angela Hampton), 15 (Angela Hampton), 18 (Angela Hampton), 20 (Angela Hampton).